Untamed spaces

Daily readings to inspire your deep and infinite nature

Shelley Hawkins, MS

ISBN: 979-8-9900162-0-0

"Nobody does what Shelley does. When it comes to eliminating your limitations and moving into your potential, Shelley's way is powerful, dependable, accurate and consistently leaves me feeling light, connected to myself and greater possibilities. My life has changed dramatically."

— Tracy Sidell, Realtor

"I wanted to let you know how much I look forward to and thoroughly enjoy your 'Monday Wisdoms'. You give all who subscribe countless pearls of wisdom and thought that, for me, give me pause for a deeper sense of connection, thought, and possible action.

They give me a sense of peace within that allows me to be more grounded in what is and how I am at the moment. You have helped me move away from self-judgment and into calm, to be more of who 'Paul' is.

What I want most for you to know is just how appreciative I am to know you. Your presence in my life has made an extraordinary difference in my ability to move with and through life with more ease. Thank you!!"

— Paul Sunderland, Ski Instructor

"I set aside time to read your Monday Wisdoms. I gain so much and they are that valuable to me."

— Carla Ferrara, Functional Nutritionist

"There is so much there that about a week later I go, 'Oh, that's what she was saying!'"

— Merle Hyatt, Carpenter

What is an untamed space? It is the unknown, the quantum, the undomesticated, unlimited, and infinite. Your dreams are not made by another version of the same thing in you. They are made by who you must become to live them and that is found in the untamed, unearthed, untapped, as yet unexpressed ever-greater versions of you ready to take form at your beckoning.

In 2014, a friend of mine invited me to a ceremony that her Unity Church did every New Year's Day, called the white stone ceremony. During this meditative ceremony we were instructed to ask for guidance on the theme of our life for the year. Whatever came, we were to write on the stone and keep it for the year.

Untamed Sparks is what I heard that morning. I could see sparks coming from multiple directions guiding me on my way that year and that even if it seemed random and wild at the time, trust that it would fit together in wholeness. Later that year, in August of 2014, I wrote the poem *Untamed Places* for my *Monday Wisdoms* online readership inspired by that Sunday morning.

In 2023, as I compiled *Monday Wisdoms* from over the years that I wanted to include in this first volume, I knew the title would appear. And it did. When I came across *Untamed Places*, I knew it was the theme of this book, my work as well as my life. I edited the *Monday Wisdom* to *Untamed Spaces*, however, which seemed even more expansive and in keeping with my experience of the infinite. "Places" felt like there were still lines being drawn around what was possible.

Soon, the photo I had taken one serendipitous evening in March of 2022 also felt fitting for the cover. The great blue herons were unusually numerous that sunset night and these two were vying for the real estate of that piling in the untamed spaces of nature.

It is like this, when the finite within and around us meets with the infinite and we have the opportunity to let go and open to something unknown within, to be inspired and upgraded beyond what we thought we could be—again and again.

Your deep and infinite nature, though it may sound serious, is not just a somber wake, as one of my *Monday Wisdoms* describes, it is also an ecstatic adventure. The more of ourselves we inspire and transmute into our infinite nature, the more of that ecstatic adventure we experience.

May it be so for you. That the molecules of the finite are transmuted by and infused with the infinite you, weaving this world in just such a way. ~By Shelley Hawkins

WATCH THE VIDEO:

Introduction to *Untamed Spaces*
http://theselfconnection.com/untamed-spaces

In the untamed spaces inside ourselves,
we find the sparks where imagination
and our grandest dreams have not tread.
Even our imaginations
are part of our domestication,
trained by what we know and will dare for.
In the mystery of our deepest fears
and our greatest ecstasies is
our new work, a new beginning,
a new love, a new idea.
Once elusive now wants to come, and will come,
from an untamed space.
Like a comet from the void lighting across your sky.
All of life seeks to wake you up for these potentials.

Either-Or is way too small for you.
This or that,
Here or there.
Go for the And, the et., the All
Where infinite possibilities await,
To collapse into your new realities
Have the bravery not to force a sequel
Of what has been.
Learn action without force
Creativity without compulsion
Knowing without confining
The life that pulls you toward it.

Wonder. Wonder.
Wonder the ache and ecstasy that led you here
Where your edges dare you
To the unknown
Where the path is not yet illumined
In Winter's reflective light
Come, step past the edge you know
Jump! And feel life underneath you
Whether in darkness or light
And let the edge now become your center
Wonder
Wonder the vastness that life holds for you
Where your edges dare you
To the unknown,
To know yourself again.

The genuine in you
Is not something you can reach for,
Act as if, achieve,
Or even fully mask.
Your genuine self silently bellows
Like an ever-burning dare,
A sweet beckoning,
To drop veil after veil.
Revealing
Who has been there all along.

You knew your dream by heart
You thought
You thought you knew your dream
By Heart
Then you walked by
And like a book
Your dream falls off the shelf
At your feet
The dream you thought you carried
Carried you
With a life of its own
Shaping and being shaped
Bigger than you could hold
'Til Now.
'Til Now.

Knowing your purpose
Is a conversation
With your own infinity
Within your finiteness.

Holding both
Shakes us loose
From the confines
Of what we think must be done
And identities of ourselves
We are sure must be true
But are not.

What is true is so much better
Simpler. Profound.

When we move out of sync with it
We find ourselves anxious.

When we know it,
We make ourselves available
To the wildness
Of our own lives.

Perhaps what you are trying to create
Doesn't want to be created
In the form, the orbit, you are trying to make it live;
And there is nothing lacking.
But a quantum sliver,
A forgotten atom
Of you
Left by grace outside of time
Campaigning for a new orbit
Existence
And conversation
With you.

Breathe deeper, lighter
Inhale to fill every rib
Every cell
And atom of your life,
Yourself, yet unlived.
Notice how life takes you in
And aspire to exhale,
To be more of who you are here to become
Settle in
To the space
That is already yours
Waiting to be inhabited by you
By you
Carbon dioxide and oxygen exchange
Take your breath
Give it back
Soak in what already is
Let life take it away again
Only to give it back again.
Live and breathe yourself into the fabric of the universe.

Live in sweet astonishment
of your very existence.

Creativity is making what was once your edge
Your new Center.
To greet the formlessness of uncertainty again
And again,
And again,
Using your imagination, courage, and emotional vastness
To be the seed—the seed—of what happens next.

Sometimes the boldest step we can take
is to step out the door and play.
When we do, we let go of the way we have been told,
or told ourselves, to experience the world,
how we are to get "stuff" done,
and we invite in timelessness and connection.

When you trust yourself with play, you trust yourself with
a bigger vision of what can occur in your life.

Teach yourself new ways of intentionally enjoying your life
and your creativity will soar.

Becoming yourself is solitary, and it's communal
A sober wake and an ecstatic dance
Reflections will show you who you are not, and who you are
Both will scare you and elate you, anger and disappoint
Make you peaceful, and make you belly laugh.
Let both build your trust, your ever-loving dare
To keep becoming.

Two people from contrasting journeys walk through the crowds
until they hear a language like their own.

Friendship is born.

They look into the eyes that mirror themselves, a stranger who knows,
recognizes them, even better at times than they know themselves,
and casts a grander reflection into the world of who they are here to be.

Imagination is multidimensional
And draws its life from the ground in us
Where something else has died
And fulfilled its purpose.
When we resist the death
We resist our own life.
When we can honor the death
We can trust ourselves with the birth of what has never been.

Before you lift a finger to contribute,
to serve,
to make an impact,
to do good,
to get involved,
to achieve,
to leave a legacy,
to build a business,
To whatever...
You are enough.
You are the service.
Your existence is the gift.
Your becoming is the point.

Step out of the half-closed door.
'Cuz love is waitin' for ya.

The best in you is born
In the convergence of seeming opposites.
Structure and Fluidity
Stillness and Momentum
Surrender and Decision
Emptiness and Abundance
Infinity and the Finite
Beauty and Starkness
Loss and Fullness
the Wild and Domestic
Power and Whimsy;
Where you have access to all of you
And avoid none of you.

There is no age limit to play.

Who you are is the gift,
the service,
the impact,
and the contribution;
What you do is the vehicle.

Let love go.
Let love in.
Death and Rebirth
All in one breath.

Everything casts a shadow
when you shine light on it;
The light reveals the shadow,
And the shadow makes the light more evident.

For a moment, suspend your disbelief and then your belief,
And then your perception, and your judgment,
Of the way things are or are not
And simply let life amaze you.
Now you're connected with who you are.

You can be in the unknown
and still be certain.

Either way,
in the eye of the calm or in the storm,
Where you are is perfect
for where you are headed
You can change it as you wish.

Creative thresholds ask what are you going to leave behind?
And what are you going to take with you?

Travel light, yes. And honor what has been.
Not all that is material is simply stuff.
And not all that is ethereal is worth keeping.

Creative thresholds ask if you are going to push life in a certain direction?
Or collaborate with your own soul?
Are you going to hang on for dear security or trust the simplicity
of the luminaries lighting your adventure?

Hero's journeys, cash flow, branding,
ecstatic vistas and dark nights,
creative expression and creative voids,
gifts and weaknesses,
solitude and collaboration,
necessity and idealism,
partnerships and dissolutions,
liberation and stagnation,
and the greatness of the true self
all invite us to shed who we are not and liberate who we are—
new dimensions of what is already within us—
and simply do what we love.

Because we love.

Change is beginnings and endings merged as one.
So if you think you have arrived,
You have.
Breathe. Dance wildly. Sleep deep. Laugh rich.
Whatever it takes to soak it in
AND make sure your body knows it actually happened.
If you think you're letting go,
Please do.
Breathe. Dance wildly. Be still. Laugh rich.
Soul, mind, and body.
And welcome yourself to your next frontier.

Your internal compass tells you where you are
And the direction you are pointed.
The steps are revealed in the stepping.

The choices you make now
Are the ancestors of your future magic.
A future that is not "out there"
It is here, moment by moment.

Your passion isn't somewhere else,
In something else, about something else or
Someone else.
Your passion is a life force within you.
Always
In your grief and in your joy
In your fervor, apathy, and your nothingness
With your friends and with your enemies
It is your awareness.
Choose what touches it.
Choose who touches it.
Know it.
Invest your whole heart to
Stand for, make time for, radiate
Your Passion, what makes you come alive.

When you trust the empty space,
In your mind,
your house,
your heart,
your time,
your relationships,
your direction;
The real thing,
The peace,
The idea,
The way,
The person,
The place,
The Flow,
The life that wants you as much as you want it,
Has the room to flow IN.

If you're doing what thrills you
And you're in integrity with your heart
You're serving.
Go forth and thrill.

If you trusted your heart right now
Would you use the same words,
Take the same action,
Think the same thought?

The physics of change
are in your favor.

I leafed through the pages of my dad's junior high textbook, fanning the pages like one does, looking for handwritten notes, slips of paper left to mark a spot, and surprise treasures. Inside the front cover, in his handwriting on the copyright page, was this:

"How to Solve a Problem:"
1. You've got to have one.
2. Find out exactly what the problem wants to know.
3. Find out what you have to work with.
4. Have a hazy idea of where to head and how.
5. Do something about it.

Physics was his favorite subject. Who knows if a teacher said this in a lecture or if he read it in a book? But it had meaning enough for him to inscribe it here, as he was known to do with thoughts that struck a chord. What fascinates me is that this is very much how he operated and his humor. I felt like I'd found one of the factors that influenced, or at least reflected, his thinking at a young age.

The five steps above, even though my dad wasn't metaphysical, describe a metaphysical approach to life as much as a practical mechanical approach to a physical puzzle. Our first step to a solution to anything, toward the physics of change, is the awareness that we've got a problem, a puzzle to be solved.

To solve a problem, you've got to have one. Awareness! Or a "this is what's happening now" approach. What's happening now could be a desire to expand or change, such as your emotional response to a situation, a belief system, or a history handed down to you. Perhaps a service in your business needs tweaking to match the mission of your company. It could be an income level you find happening year after year, a pattern you intend to surpass. A desire to take your longtime relationship into even more joy and connection. A way of eating that isn't getting your desired results. A way of giving without also having your needs met.

Awareness happens in meditation, relationships, dreams, masterminds, reading and learning, mentoring, traveling, solitude, contemplation, walks, and play, for example.

Find out what the problem wants to know. Not you. The problem. The way this one is worded is perhaps my favorite. In other words, get out of your way and listen. Connect with your puzzle! Tune in. The problem, or puzzle if you prefer, is its own energy just as you are, your business or what you do in life, your relationship, and every thought you have.

What is the problem, the new idea, the expansion, the crises, the opportunity telling you when you're still enough to ask and listen? What greater possibility or probability is it pointing to? Eureka's, healings, everyday miracles, and bliss happen in connection.

Drop out of your head into the magnetic field of your physical heart to get a more accurate response than your brain. It may come to you in a flash or in the days to come when your mind is relaxed or focused on something else. Solutions often come in the middle of the night. That bathroom run may not just be for your bladder!

You may discover that what you thought was an expense is a wise investment in your future. That cutting ties liberates oceans of creativity for your purpose and a life filled with love. That a small inventory of houses is the beginning of a new level of creative expression. That writing your book teaches you what you needed to learn and the audience is your companion.

Find out what you have to work with. Are you a MacGyver lost in the woods and need to build a shelter with a toothpick and some moss? Are you trying to move mountains with doubt instead of faith, or while packing a pile (or a sliver) of unresolved energetic/emotional habituation instead of liberation and an expanded perspective?

Consider your internal and external environment in what you have to work with. Do you have people who proactively love and support you, and who have your back? Are you in a "room" (in your head, in an institution, a social circle) of passives and life-suckers, like trying to fill a bathtub with the drain open?

Get it out on the table. Whatever your puzzle or problem, what do you have to work with? When you have it in front of you and you keep your mind open, inspiration starts taking over. That toothpick and moss might look like a thrilling challenge. Behold, the MacGyver in you!

If you're building a relationship, are you proactively growing yourself as part of your contribution? Are you allowing your needs to be met? Are you living from the habits of relationships gone by? If you're building a company or an empire, where are your strengths, your people capital, your gifts capital as well as the holes in your strategy?

Having a hazy idea of where to head and how makes me laugh. I can see Dad's furrowed brow in my memories' eye, with greasy hands, while weeding the garden or sitting at the kitchen table sketching a drawing, 'til he got an inkling of something to try on whatever he was fixing.

Even when we have a mapped-out strategy, we rarely know more than the next step (the parameters shift with every move) and even that can be hazy. A hazy idea, an inkling, is enough! Life is an experiment, not a test.

Do something about it. The power of our thought, our intentions, our meditations, our ideas, our values, our beliefs, our inventions, and our hearts, must be followed by personal action. That hazy idea needs feet. Courage. Liberation. Get 'er done.

Plug the drain of that bathtub and soak in the rise in your creativity. Start with a phone call to get a question answered. Meditate. Sign the document. Stop saying yes. Hire a few hours of help. Meditate. Download the app. Send a voice text of love. Set boundaries. Rent an Airbnb treehouse for solitude and creative space—a new environment to sit and do nothing, for new perspective and inspiration, to write, to start working out, to revel.

The physics of change can be passively endured or actively (intentionally) engaged. If the latter, then your toothpick and moss will look like a miracle waiting to happen. It's all in your favor.

Here's to brilliant change directed by you.

On that shore of what seems practical to ask, will often be
the question hiding in the waves crashing at your feet ...
"Who am I to...?"

Cooperate
with your Inner Wisdom.

We become the future
We inhabit in the present moment.

LIVE
Like your heart can't break.
On the other side of
Every invisible barrier
Is more bliss
And another batch of courage.

Shine your light
Where it can ricochet

Tell a different story.
Write your own myth.

You're the reason
Dawn Breaks
Every morning.

You've lived your whole life
Preparing for this moment,
This next phase of life.
Look at the magnificence before you.

Life regenerates itself constantly,
Toward more light.
It is harder to try
To maintain status quo
Than to choose to move
Into your greater potentials.

Enthusiasm
is contagious, too.

Whatever is falling apart
Is making more room
For your wings.

Your Influence is delivered
in the way you hold your perspective.

The past sometimes repeats itself
Like phantom pains
Give them the attention they deserve
Which is the wisdom you have now
From a past that no longer exists.
Receive whatever it has left to offer you,
including passing on by.

Old Structures Out,
Love In.

In every interaction
We have the opportunity
to be a place of Increase.

Group think can mean you lose yourself in a majority;
Or it can be a creative and purposeful act of synergy
by those with a moving vision for a beautiful world.

Peace before you
Peace behind you
Peace outside
Peace inside
Peace be restful
Peace be fierce
Peace fill you
Peace free you
Peace protect you
Peace reveal you.

Life speaks in symbols;
It's code for love.

Love Wins.
All of these—joy, magic, power, hope, love—
Are your sovereign belongings.

One of the fascinating aspects of quantum reality and understanding your human life in that context is that it does not move in one direction. For example, the intentions you have today, the thoughts and feelings you cast from your reel of creation, also affect your past and your future. To restate, your present intentions, change your past. They change your future. They change your present.

In fact, multiple studies demonstrate that our future is influencing our present. And our present is influencing our past. We think this is strange because we believe in time. It seems that we march linearly from cause to affect all day every day. You made this plan and x happened. Someone said this and y happened.

"Time does not exist," said Einstein (and many more scientists in agreement) we invented it. Time is what the clock says. The distinction between the past, present and future is only a stubbornly persistent illusion."

If you can wrap your heart, soul, and intellect around this, it means that you in your individual life, and we in this collective life, are constructing and reconstructing life as we know it all day every day. Heaven on earth, hell on earth, flatlined on earth.

You are not stuck. This world is not stuck. Are there dark forces in play? Attitudes we encounter? Sure. Life is way more Harry Potter-esk, metaphorically speaking, than we realize with forces inside and out that want to suck the joy out of you, your power, hope, and magic. And those forces often gain their so-called power by conveying the belief that there is no other way.

There's a way. Infinite possibilities, in fact.

I was speaking with a colleague and friend the other day who was deeply discouraged from some news she had received. She couldn't see a solution yet. She needed to sit with the shock of the event first and let the solution show itself. But she was affirming a new way forward, a solution, writing down intention for her way forward, what she wished to create in light of recent events, even while she was absorbing how the latest events felt like they had destroyed her previous plans.

"We are essentially living in one smeared out now," said Lynne McTaggart in her many books and a recent article. (https://lynnemctaggart.com/when-intention-goes-backward/) Lynne has provided us so much accessible science on the effect our attitudes have on each other physically, mentally, emotionally and spiritually. (See her book, *The Bond*) And the power our intention plays in creating this world.

The intention my friend puts forward now will create her future as well as change her past and allow the future to change her past and present.

When a land is plundered, because of life's movement in all directions, you can be sure there is a new beginning at hand. It is the constant theme in transformational stories. Not horror stories. The hero and the heroine's journey. The Hobbit, Harry Potter, Star Wars, Snow White.

So-called fairy tales are symbolically describing awakenings. Awakenings to love, to new life, to overcoming darkness within and out, and discovering a refreshingly beautiful world. Prince Charming and Sleeping Beauty, Frodo Baggins in Middle Earth, and so on. They are metaphors for a principle of life we always have at hand.

But these new beginnings don't just happen. They are chosen. They are chosen by reminding ourselves continually that love wins. Or we can believe the reverse and have that experience instead.

In my friend's situation, she must look into her own heart to where love guides her now. Leaving for good what now feels like a plundered land and into what awaits her. This same idea plays out for all of us on a global level. We can hold collective intentions for what we fear or for what we love.

"Above all else, be the heroine (hero) of your own life and not the victim." — Nora Ephron, Movie Director

You are finite and infinite
Learning to live in both as
One instrument.

Allow yourself to be carried
Beyond the plans you've made.

Dance with Life as your partner
Not your parent!

Joy is a universal truth.
You may have to move a few things
Out of your universe to access it.
But it's always there.

What you learn from history
You can use to make history.

The difference you make on this planet
Lights up significantly
As you move your creative motivation
From necessity, crises, and fear
To tending your evolution by
Leading and authoring your life.

If you hit the snooze button
And fall asleep
Infinity will do its best
To wake you back up.

To make magic, you don't necessarily have to believe it exists. Most days I come across someone who is being magical, whether they realize it or not. And the ones who don't realize it can be the most fun.

"We are made to hold infinity," said Brian Andreas in his simple and inspirational book, *Songs of Starlight*.

"All you need to do, he says whimsically, to have a magical life:

1. Stop hiding

2. Seriously, stop hiding. No more lies. No more secrets. No more being addicted to what people think. (Warning!! Do not read #3 until after you do this. Even though you & I both know you will. But it won't do you any good. Oh well. Go ahead.)

3. You never aren't in a magical life. So yeah. Now go back and start with #1."

There are many ingredients to a magical life, of course. Why does it matter? So that we are creating a world where spirit and matter, the mystical and physical, the magical and practical, thrive as one. From the boardroom to the bedroom.

So that we are not checking our humanity and all its possibilities at the door of our workplace, or our parenthood, or classroom, or hospitable room, or in any relationship, leaving some part of ourselves behind and out of the equation. If we diminish our own humanity, we are by extension in some way diminishing that of others.

Practicality is fine and good. But we've all experienced the feeling, for example, at a basketball game where whatever tipped the ball into the net in the last second of overtime can't be explained.

We need the unexplainable to light us up, to move us into our optimum, into our infinities.

At one time it was thought that the brain you were born with was the brain you die with. Now we know, thanks to research results for about the last decade, that the brain is neuro-plastic. Meaning, we are constantly changing the structure of our brain and therefore our bodies and lives, with every thought, feeling, choice, experience, energetic transformation, and all that we learn, unlearn and reinforce.

You can transform your brain (https://www.youtube.com/watch?v=ELpfYCZa87g) from trauma, rigidity, or bitterness for example to bliss, safety, creativity, and teach yourself and choose environments where you can sustain such states. The videos demonstrating under a microscope how quickly, often instantly, our synapses change, for example through meditation, are fascinating.

You are constantly making, reinforcing, or trimming synapses in your brain that reinforce a perspective, a trauma, love, safety, creativity, disease, prosperity or health, for example. When I am working with people, these synapses are transforming constantly.

More from Brian's book… "I want to learn magic, I said. Where do I start? My grandfather looked up from the book he was reading. Stop learning all the stuff that's not magic, he said. It'll be easier than having to forget it all later."

Magic often flashes through a moment, moving sparks around and between people, words, and events. Then bounces on to the next willing vessels. It is also a learnable way of being. Magic is one of those controversial words that people love to love, or love to hate. I've chosen it purposely, of course, for that reason.

Its taboo is its gift, though, helping it move about unimpeded, finding willing hearts (and brains), touching in to change a situation and moving on. You can call it by a name that feels more palatable to you and unwoo—a logical course of events, a mindset, luck, serendipity, grace, providence, good fortune, a job well done, an answer to prayer, synchronicity, your guardian angel, peace, lack of resistance....

By whatever name you call it, it moves the brain into states that change your life.

We are all holograms of a greater self. That greater self shines from within—and out— through the perspectives and experiences we hold like the filtered light of sun through the leaves of the trees. It's rays land with the shape they've filtered through.

Your greater self is as constant as the sun, seeking expression, and using the data that it moves through within you to shape its expression. It's completely unconditional! So why not go for the gold?

Magic, by whatever name you call it, is there to help you let go of your littleness. To send it down river into the ocean of transmutation where it is picked up again to rain on you with freshness and delight. Or to shape it into a sunlight-through-the-trees self that lights your way.

Magic is never not there for you. You were made for these infinities.

"To attain knowledge, add things every day.
To attain wisdom, remove things every day."
— Lao Tzu

Nothing is too good to be true.
We're simply navigating doubt and possibilities,
truth and falsehood,
to learn a bigger love.

Ego love allows us all,
Including you,
To experience the best of you.
Egotism is the smokescreen
For the self a person doesn't have.
Ego love is the sanctuary
For a soul fully expressed.

No matter how big
The contrast
Grow brighter still.

And still...
light prevails.

Perhaps this is a time of greater light brilliantly eclipsed in a challenge. To grow the glow around you and your highest potentials. For you to grow more nimble in a changing world, shrug off the attachments to the old shore and find yourself in rarified air with other stars that can't wait to shine with you.

Joy is the constant;
like a homing signal
Reminding us of our natural calibration.

Be a vehicle for miracles.

What if it is not our britches
We are too big for,
And it's
our britches
That no longer fit who we've become?

Firecrackers and children both have potential;
It depends on how you light them up!

There's a child in you that, thankfully, never grows up. He or she keeps us accountable to ourselves, our joy, our true needs, our playfulness because therein lies our potential.

The child will guide you to your wounds as well as to your ecstasy because, like any child, she wants to flow, to be in motion. To feel what he feels, have it validated and be done with it. To feel safe, secure, understood, and celebrated. To discover what she can do. To be held. To play.

It's pretty simple. He wants to cry when he's hurt, scared, or sad; laugh when something is funny, get every need met. She wants to feel the security of love and boundaries and play all day long.

Your child self, or inner children, hold a key to your latent potentials and what you have yet to bring forward in this life. When your adult self is saying, this is too good to be true, your child self is saying, are you kidding me? This is just getting good!

A client said to me the other day, "I did everything I was supposed to. I've been putting money into retirement funds; I have a great job with a sizable income. I got married. I had kids. Somewhere along the way I got lost in the day to day. I forgot how to dream. To know what I really want and set goals for my future."

It's easy to get on with what must be done as you move through adulting. Earning a living, finishing school, raising kids, making friends, building a business, getting involved, and forgetting about the gaps and wounds in your childhood. That is, until you meet them in a relationship, in an inability to say yes to opportunity, a disease, a financial challenge, and flatness for a life you used to love.

By design, your child inside is still connected to dreams, fairytales, and so-called fantasies. Yours. You will need her to be a great leader. You will need him to set goals that mean something to you. To make the most of yourself.

Those pieces that seem lost of yourself, or out of reach, can be gathered at any time, though you may need to rebuild trust. It's never—ever—too late. Time is an illusion. We're working in the Field, in energy, which knows no time or space. And those things that bring the gaps and wounds to your attention, are the best thing that ever happened to your potential.

If you determine the "why" you hold behind any intention and keep drilling down, eventually you will get to something along these lines: to be happy; to experience life; to love your life; to be comfortable/abundant, to be free, to live your potential or make the most of yourself.

Every intention you set is for the living of more life, which children are full of, and to express and experience something more in yourself. The child in you will help you do that. That is, if her needs are met. If he feels protected, heard, and free and gets to play.

You need the wisdom and life experience of your adult-self working with the playful, dreamy, fantasies of your child-self. Because somewhere in there is the alchemy of your latent potentials. The wounded child isn't meant to stay wounded and needs the adult self to have the courage and commitment to transform, to go for the gold.

Your inner child will have as much to say as your adult self about your next move in your profession or business, guiding your sales team, where to live, your relationships, or guiding your student to success.

Where would you be if a key adult in your childhood hadn't given what you needed at that time? Now imagine a timeline where you had everything you needed to thrive.

This week, consider playing with this:

* Invite your inner child to speak. Invite them into your heart. Does he or she trust you? If not, why not? Are you ready to change that? If he or she does trust you, then let's carry on!

* Ask your child self what it wants to do about your next career/business decision or any decision you have on your mind at the moment. The response may change your parameters for decision making…and bring you into alignment with yourself.

* Ask your child self how to love someone in your life better. You may be moved to deeper vulnerability, creativity, spontaneity, and more playfulness.

* Ask your child self about your current daily rhythm. What would he or she do differently. Will you listen and act? blow it off?

How much of your potential do you want to live? 20%? 50%? 100%? Set the intention in this moment to live there now. Ask your child what it has to say about your potential. And as the adult, take action.

Everything your life has been;
Becomes your Genius.

Ideas are like adventures
Looking for the one crazy enough
To say yes.

Your
Deepest
Aspirations
Deserve
You.

Fearlessness is fueled by peace.

Hair-on-fire fearlessness can be fun. But to sustain your fire, its well is filled with inner peace. If Maslow had stopped at safety as our need, we would all be left on the edge waiting for something else to unhinge us. Safety by nature is safe from something. We must move deeper and broader than safety to experience our authentic boldness, fearlessness and ultimate peace.

Power well lived
Is Reciprocal.

Keep waking up,
You're on a roll!

Be a Fool for the love
Of your own life.

Give what you decide to give.

Give your liberation a purpose;
Freedom is as much a portal to choose something greater
as it is a freedom from where you've been.

Prioritize
What puts you in the Zone.

Creating your day is your masterpiece.
Where it goes from there is the adventure!

Designing your life
Takes a whole lot of love.

Life is an experiment,
Not a test!

Raise the vibe.
Raise the roof.
Raise the stakes.
Raise the grain.
Sand it down again.
Raise your sights.
Rock the boat.
Make waves.
Make ripples.
Make joy.
Bring it from your heart.
Make it real.
You're the one.

Imagination and Action
Are like DNA
A symbiotic ladder
Into New Creations;
Malleable at anytime
By Consciousness.

When we see
The miracle in everything
We are connecting with our greatness.

Could You Believe
in a
Greater-Yet-To-Be?

The more infinity you participate with,
The more of that infinity you draw into
and through your life.
Everything responds to the energy you attach to it.

We are swimming in infinity with unlimited creativity at the fingertips of who we become in the physical world. If that gives you superlative fatigue, consider this. No matter how great any one person becomes, there is still more for everyone, for you.

It may look like money is only going one direction when you're spending it, but it is an energy circulating as much as the love you shower on your beloved. Everything responds to the energy you attach to it.

Instead of thinking of settling for enough,
How about stepping off the plateau
Into the unlimited?

Don't just hope for it;
Become it!

In everything you do
Convey increase.

If we live in a state of increase for the sake of increase, we become like a cancer cell, where our multiplication comes with our own demise or sacrifice of wholeness. If we make our increase part of an intentionally creative life, a loving life, becoming more ourselves, we give our cells and every other part of our life and people in it new information. A new consciousness from which to create and regenerate.

Announcement:
Infinity is ready to move in
To as much of your humanity as you desire.
May cause littleness to dissolve.

If everything you need
is within you,
It drives home the primal point
To take care of yourself;
To be passionate about creating
An environment inside and out
Where you naturally thrive.

Hold a vision worthy of pulling you forward;
A greater reality behind your eyes
Than what you see in front of them.

Purpose is how you do anything.

Cherish More.

* What do you cherish?
* Whom do you cherish?
* How do you cherish?
* How do you act on it?
* What scares you about cherishing?
* What inspires you about cherishing?
* How can you make this your own?
* Will you let it change you?

On this side of a window of possibility
your choice looks deceivingly small;
On the other side
You will hardly remember who you use to be.

May the elixir
of Thanks-Giving
permeate your life.

There is something grand that beats our hearts, that moves and animates each
of us that cannot be defined. Not by science. Not by religion. Not by philosophy.
And thankfully so because defining it would diminish it to something we think we
understand. Though I love language, words, and communication, this is experienced.
By living.

Allow.
Allow yourself to invest
In your uncompromised and continually morphing dreams.
Allow the details to fall into place.

Make Way
for more
Awe.

Only the Unknown
Can guarantee the unlimited;
Follow the awe.

Unprecedented times
Shake up the energy for use
In any direction.
Optimism, enthusiasm, groundedness,
Hope, vision, cheer, joy, and the like
Are Contagions, too.

We always have the option
to tune to channels that lower our frequency
or raise them.

Evolutionary change
Doesn't leave anything
To go back to.

May the oases in your life
Multiply.

Allowing yourself to be known
Is part of the adventure
Choosing who to be in it with you
Is part of the wisdom.

Uncertainty and Adventure
Are the same thing.

We're all teetering on the ledge
Of another frontier of greatness,
Love that draws you home from your future.

Give me the unknown
With its infinities...
The finite of the known
Is just too small a life;
I'd rather give my all
To the love of mastery
Than settle for safety.

Be an architect of the impossible.

Love fierce
Love fluffy
Love peaceful
Love boundaried
Love untamed
Love crazy
Love undomesticated
Love simply
Love silly
Love steady
Love quietly
Love boldly
Love silently
Love hilariously
Love powerfully
Love.

In any moment
You Calibrate
Toward contraction
Or expansion.

Invest your Now.

Leave the gap for sparks to occur
For light to fill in the fractures and fissures
For more of you to come alive.

Whatever happened,
Power alone didn't do it.
True power is
An aspect of wholeness.

The lure of strategy
Can pull us off our
Intuitive Game;
Keep strategy in service
to your intuition.

Transcend a lifetime
Of what you are not;
Transcendence doesn't need a past.
It's all in service to your fire within.

What moves you forward today?
What do you choose to be moved by?
Joy?
Desire?
Gratitude?
Vision?
Potential?
Bliss?
Peace?

You could wait to live at depth
Or you could live there now;
You could wait to be a philanthropist until you have millions
Or you could be one now with whatever you have;
You could wait till you're dead to leave a legacy
Or you could live one now;
You could treat time like a limitation
Or you could expand time in all its dimensions, now.

Cast
Nobility
Into your future.

Contentment
is excellent fuel
for creating more.

Attend to your
Joy.

It's time we see ourselves as what we are. Consciousness (soul, awareness) bringing matter (physical stuff and experience) into being. Rather than as matter (something physical) having some extraordinary epiphany of consciousness.

When we do, see ourselves this way that is, attending to our joy will not be a self-care task list. Or an egoic focus on me and me-time. It will be our way of life. A thirst for more joy, love, infinite creativity moving through us. A commitment to letting go of what and who is not. An attentiveness to our daily energy hygiene for living our potentials. And our lists will become what we choose to do from our joy.

There's something amazing
Waiting for you
In every area of your life
On the other side of
Your next barrier to love.

What you have created so far
Is a fraction
of what lies latent,
within you.

Let your intuitive awareness
Pierce your logic
Letting the air out
Of a worn-out perspective;
Leading you home
To uncharted territory.

Heart open
Boundaries clear
Body relaxed
Love on ~
I dare you.

Use the energy of chaos
Like a propulsion
To move you
As the eye of the storm.

May your year be expansive and intimate
Rooted and elevated.
Inspiring and thought provoking.
May you discover new ways to play
And see beauty where you haven't noticed before;
May this year compost, nourish and launch the next
May you laugh hard and your sorrows open new doors.
May your joys compound
And your bliss move you.
May multiplicity govern your potentials
May your adventurous spirit feel the thrill of being alive
May your imagination become new realities
May the light that you are
Transform the darkness of the world.
Let there be light...Yours.

Let go of what isn't love and
Courageously, enthusiastically
Leave the space for what is love
To take its place.

I blinked. "Business is inherently selfish," he said. I paused to see if he actually meant it. He did. The conversation went on for a bit, ending with our differing views expressed kindly. Then we headed back for the dance floor.

I go more for the Kahlil Gibran version of business, "...work is love made visible". There's plenty of soulless work in the world.

But not in my world. Not in yours.

Where are you holding what isn't love, what isn't alive to you?

Breathe it out. Dissolve it. Become unrecognizable to it. Move your attention.

Love the space and it will love you back.

A new epoch of your life
Can spark from a single idea.
Is it the one you're having now
Or now...or now...?

Your will is as powerful
As the connection
That governs it.

You are wired to be
extraordinary.

Imagine all the reasons
Why you can.

Remember your future.

Security, ironically,
is an act of great risk,
Called Trust.

I am my wholeness
I am my ideas
I am my shadows
I am my fire
I am my gentleness
I am my fear
I am my insight
I am my courage
I am my vitality
I am my peace
I am my art
I am my ego
I am my soul.
And I am none of it
Because I am beyond all of it.

The winds of life bend us into proportions we don't recognize
So that when we are upright again
It is no longer our only standard.
Here comes another gust.
Bend!

Everything casts a shadow when you shine light on it;
Relationships, ideas, trees, beliefs, dogs, people, purpose, gifts, boats.
The light is the point. It's how life reveals what comes next.

The Art of Nourishment is
Regenerative.
Let's take it beyond filling up
Getting ready for the next thing
Superficial or transient self-care and other-care.
To a philosophy and intentionality
Of Regeneration.
Elevating each cell into greater vitality
For the long haul and the deep dive
For sustained joy, raucous laughter, and sublime tears.
Each cell of your body, yes,
And each cell of humanity, your relationships, the soil;
Your business, your classroom, your tribe.
Cleanse, detoxify, declutter
Fuel, fill up, care. Yes.
But more,
Rest. Nourish. Dare yourself out of action. Love.
Regenerate.

Wholeness gives us the power
To rekindle our fire into new directions.
We can retreat into our wholeness to access the fire
That never goes out
That waits for us to listen
To the simplicity of what we value.
It's as powerful in question as in clarity
Whatever transition you are in,
A new platform of light
A dark hole
Whatever is challenging you to become more of who you already are
Let your soul saturate you.

Let my creativity now spark the life in others
So brilliantly, so gently, so palpably
That they never again forget who they are.
And what I give, I receive.

Keep your dreams lucid
They are the language of your heart
Moving you
In a direction
To wake you up to yourself;
As your presence ironically sharpens in lucidity
With the language of your own deep, light, and true desire,
Your aim grows clear, focused, and directed.
And you hit the mark of your soul's bullseye.

Who you're being is your work in the world
What you do is the vehicle
Your presence will make the world a better place
Move an idea forward
Transform another toward their greater yet to be
Doctor, carpenter, parent, or cook
Your presence exists before the vehicle called your work.
Cultivate That.

The genuine in you is what the world longs to see
Even when they don't know it.
The one with nothing to prove,
Nothing to strategize,
But who listens for your listening;
Where you and your true desires meet.
Where questions melt and miracles are made.
And meaning just is.
Are you listening?

Joy

Where do we source our joy from?
Joy comes from the depths
When we stop running from our own true gifts,
Or chasing our significance.

Joy roots us and thrives us,
So the winds of ecstasy and grief are both welcome
As they move with reverence through our leaves and branches unimpeded.

Joy is meaning in our every moment because we know
Our very existence is its own purpose.

Resistance is waking you up to a new optimum.

Enjoy the voyage as it is now
So you can reminisce about it later.

Play in the invisible, where all possibilities take their shape.
Even in a moment that seems like a debacle
Flip it in your mind into a silent intention for the outcome you intend instead
Let go, stay present, and allow life to show up for you.

Liberation...
Leaving the habits
Fears
Joys
Causes
Filters
Happinesses
Beliefs
Judgments
Nightmares
Reasons
Obsessions
Dreams
Thoughts
Comforts
Actions
That shape you, your body, your mind and your world as it is
To See, Be & Move
From the even great-er-ness of You
That is waiting to be known
By you.

Clutter disappears
When the condition inside
No longer accommodates it.

Go as far as your imagination can take you
Then let go and see what the Beyond reveals

Power grows with trust.
The more surrendered and alive you become
To your true and unique nature
The more your power trusts you
With its true expression.

Attune yourself with what wants to happen
Your deepest desires
And let the waves to particles roll.

My wings formed and stretched
I pressed from the inside
Feeling my strength
Until the cocoon opened and fell away
Just fell away.
The sun was rising behind the clouds
Like fire behind a curtain
Their edges lined with golden white, blazing orange, and fiery pinks
The dawn rose
And with it my sight
My wings were ready and the breeze
Greeted me like a cosmic playmate waiting for me to wake up
I opened my wings
And the wind came to meet me
I opened my wings
And the wind lifted me.
I opened my wings
The wind and I were one.

Adventure and terror are twin flames
Welcome them both
You may need to burn through one to feel the other
We learn the spectrum so we can come fully alive
See the terror instead of seeing from it
It's a part of you coming home
Feel it as joy burning through dross
For its next evolution
And adventure with its joy
Will greet you again
Like the friend that was with you all along

Imperceptible shifts
Are the seeds
Of exponential leaps

The arrival of what you want, unforced, isn't the solution to your problem
It's the affirmative evidence that you had already solved it.
And the Ethers are simply responding.

A book falls off the shelf
Its tattered edges remind you
Of the time you spent there
Drinking in the words
Until they were part of you
And then you placed it on the shelf
Like a dream
A Dream
You walk by
And your Dream falls off the shelf
Its tattered edges and felted pages
Remind you
Of the time you spent there
Drinking it in
And now you muse again
Is it real?
Can I?
Will I?
Do I deserve it?
Is it mine?
It's mine!

It doesn't matter how
This time
Is the time.
You move and it moves with you
And the tattered edges become the beauty
That makes every moment of incubation
The richness that feeds your new life.

Creativity & Resistance are lovers.
Seeming opposites
With the desire
To be One within you.

While you're pursuing what gives you joy
Joy pursues you.
I'm right here! I'm right here!
Come in!

Sometimes we need the boldness that bellows from a podium
That stirs us
Wakes us up to rebel,
Lays our heart open to how we feel
And sometimes we need the boldness that permeates without a word,
To be blown away with silence;
Like the power of a look that is a hand at your back.

There's almost always something we consider unchangeable.
That's the way it is, we say.
Without even realizing it, we contribute to holding 'it',
or them, or him, or her, where it is.
If you could change it, what would you want it to be instead? What would you shift?
Ditch the petty.
Imagine it now.
Go vivid. Love it.
Back from your adventure,
Did it change your perspective?
Did it change you?

Synchronicity is another word for oneness
Undivided wholeness.
Like geese in sync to each one's movement.

Leaps are so often a fractional step
We thought was too expensive
Unclear
Out of our reach
Frightening
Only to find as we step
The ground is already beneath us.
Even if in the most
unexpected
world rocking
peaceful
unpretentious
Way.

Let there be light,
Yours.

One bold act, or a succession of them,
Can pull you out by the roots.
Thankfully
Leaving you bewildered
Unable to recreate what rooted you before
Until you find yourself,
Drawing nourishment,
Laughing,
Creating,
Prospering,
Loving,
Being loved,
And Rooted
Where you couldn't have planned it any better
To be.

When you feel the restlessness of change around the bend,
Peek around the corner with your imagination to discover what you already know
And anticipate the joy of what is unknown.

We get to feel the ecstasy, flow, and filled-up-ness of our own purpose when we're no longer giving from our wounds and instead give from the wisdom gained with the energetic liberation of our genuine selves.

Raise the flag of your ragged dreams
And let the gales and gusts and simple breezes
Refresh their elegance,
Renew your expectancy,
And billow in.

We couldn't possibly imagine the capacity
Of all that we are, all at once;
That's grace.
Our lives are an experiment.
We get glimpses of our capacities
That compel us into new dimensions.
Where the angst can't exist and peaceful exhilaration is.
Creating is the evolution that happens
In our willingness to take the veils off our own eyes
To what it means to be ourselves.

Imagine your plans this week through the lenses of play;
The pleasure of the grit required in play
For the challenge
Play as your favorite way to learn
Play as perfect cross training for the unexpected
A full out contest without the competition – like squirrels or kids;
Exhilarated when you've given everything and feel completely spent.
An artesian well of creativity
Being purposely unpurposeful.
Exploration for its own sake.

Your bold creations come
From the paradox
Of what roots you
And uproots you at the same time.
Where steadiness and stillness
Weave you
With innovation and leaps.

Meet your extraordinary
Just outside the edge of your familiar
A simple inward leap
Through the fiery edge of your personal atmosphere
Past old rhythms, thought, feeling, people, stuff, goals, supposed to's;
Saturate your outer world
With the new you.

Being you is the melody
What you accomplish are the harmonizing notes.

No matter what else you do today,
Revel in meaning.
Take a walk to enjoy your world.
Spark a rich conversation and ask yourself what you can give to it.
Stretch your boundaries of bravery.
Trust life with more of you than you did yesterday.

Power is a force that you tap into more than something you have.
When you have it, you contract it, confine it, doubt it, manipulate it, wield it.
When you tap into it, you are part of it, you direct it, you surrender to it.
You are grown by it and you grow it.
And send it back into the ethers for more.

True power grows with your courage to open yourself
To the creative expression that is yours alone
And trust yourself with the power that wants to move you and that only you can move
In a work and a life that could only be yours.

You can make a difference selling light bulbs.
Simply get about the business of being you
Kindness, creative excellence, being congruent
Being present to loving what is, using your mind to create
a game from what is happening now
Everything you need is right here
For crafting what comes next.

Play educates your imagination;
Imagination is the mechanism by which you engage possibility;
Possibility becomes the reality you participate in orchestrating.

Like the earth moves unceasingly around the sun,
We can become more of ourselves – unceasingly
Shedding the silly and sacred wounds, notions, and veils that drive us;
To discover new orbits within our very selves.

There are hearts you can feel
Across the phone, the globe, the text,
The silence.
Be one of those.

Create and rest.

Resistance isn't always resistance.
Sometimes it's life saying, go a different direction.
Ease.

When you move from the mechanistic to the intuitive way of working,
You shift your source of change and creative movement.
Your work morphs, shapes and forms from inner driven action.
It's the difference between making a leap from a standing position
And having the wind lift you as you leap.
One is completely of your own effort against the force of gravity
and limited to what can be produced from your resources.
The other is limitless in possibility.
Which do you choose?

To reinvent yourself, to be available to a new beginning,
you must source yourself from a new well of passion.
What drove you before no longer exists.
To forge new possibilities, ask, "what moves me now?"

A driving passion to change the world
will seem necessary
until we heal the perspective
within ourselves.

Simplicity seems to be at the root of bliss.
No matter how complex the art, the heart, the flavor
It all synthesizes into something almost indescribable
to make that moment we call
Bliss.

Life's lumens move through you like a prism in a spectrum of color.
You need life to live and life needs you to give it expression.

Our destinies are always wooing us to create them
Potentials anticipating their own arrival
Like babies that can't wait to be born.

Who you are is the impact
Regardless of what you do.

Moving forward can also mean standing still.

Relationship is the current-cy of greatness
In relationship we become ourselves;
Like a network of currents
Within us, from us, to us
Rivers, streams, and tributaries
Meeting, weaving, and flowing
Into the ocean
To be evaporated
Drawn up
And precipitated down
To feed us, weave, and flow again.

Sometimes resistance is being blinded by your own magnificence.
Instead of pushing past it, melt into it.
You may find yourself wallowing in exactly what you craved.

Waiting for a guarantee
Is a limitation~
You are a creator
You are not a controller.
There is so much more
to receive
with a daring act
of trusting life.

What is mastery?
What does it mean to become masterful?
The most masterful people I know are present with the thing they are doing,
without need to prove themselves.
They care.
As if they enter a sacred space whether they're fixing a car,
writing a book, helping someone heal, riding a bike, steering a boat,
speaking to thousands, or planting a seedling.
Mastery isn't in the mechanics. It's in the love.
The invisible.
I've known people with great skill without mastery.
I know I'm with a master when the mechanics are invisible
and I feel a fluidness in me when I watch them.
There is no separation between them and the wrench,
the bike, the boat, the book, the audience.
And yet there resides a deep respect between the two—
animate and inanimate objects.
This oneness is the point of it all.
Of mastery.
To open yourself to still more, as if you have only just begun.

Your gift and your achilles heal walk together
The light looks light because of the dark
Until the light no longer needs it.
And is content to shine.

There is nothing new under the sun they say,
But there has never been one like you.

Be careful what you wish for?
Nah,
Hold nothing back.
High expectancy makes high magic.

Thank your fears as much as your joy
For being where you are and who you are this moment
They've been the right amount of hesitation for perfect timing
Courage to walk straight into the fire
Your compass to go a new way
Held you back for protection
Your knowing to walk away
Curiosity to open a door
Impetus to overcome
Willingness to let go.
The contrast for a new day.

You live inside the ultimate canvas.
With every choice the artist simply adjusts
To make a greater piece of art.

You think you know kindness
And the corny clichés about spreading it around
Until someone surprises you
With a genuineness so simple
So present
So empty of agenda
And so full of innocence
The light inside you leaps to attention.

You are here to become who you are
And you cannot do it by yourself
Some reflections will show you who you are not
Some reflections will show you who you are
Both will scare you, anger you, disappoint you.
Both will elate you, excite you, make you laugh.
Let both build your trust,
Your ever-loving dare
To keep Becoming.

Imagination is training your brain
Beyond its domestication
Beyond what you can "think up"
To support a new future
That will thrill you and scare you
Rest you and enbraven you.
That will take the seeds you give it
And return a vision and love
Unfamiliar yet completely at home.

Compassion is intimacy without the hook
Care without the pity
Understanding without the judgment
Infusing dignity into the suffering
Awe into the path chosen
Liberation by your presence.

No matter what has happened
You are positioned perfectly
For what comes next.

The New Purpose, your true purpose, is ancient;
To live yourself, and live yourself well.
Then give from the overflow.
We're all ready.

Intention is creative responsibility
Imagination our medium
With it, we dissolve old realities
And sculpt new ones.

Certainty is as seductive as adventure
Systems and steps woo us
Alongside the dare of the unknown.
Be the fool.
Why NOT reinvent the wheel?
Not for unnecessary effort
But to open a yet unconceived portal
From within the heart of life
A bloodstream of expression, as you,
The one you haven't met yet
To whom you have barely dared a glance
Afraid s/he is out of your league.
Be the fool.
Peacefully. Quietly. With fervor
Bold has many flavors.
Be the fool.
For the love of your own life. For others.
For life itself.

Human beings are the only species who can refuse
To be themselves.
So our journeys are to that end.
To lay down our refusal and become the life,
The love,
Our true nature,
That wants only to bring us alive
Not to cram us into the suffering confinements of being—
Being—someone else's ideal
Being—less than our genuine
Of hydroplaning on the surface of our own lives
Avoiding immersion into the only purpose that can ever exhilarate us
The sheer delight in our own Being
Of Life Itself
And the Awe of its numinous generosity to others.

Acknowledgements

These Monday Wisdoms represent a random collection of the hundreds I've written over 18 years, so my gratitude goes to so many who contributed during that time, including my own life experiences and evolution.

Thank you to my readers and clients for your inspiration. Your words of gratitude for the transformation and inspiration you experience in reading inspires more writing.

Thank you to my team for managing all things technical, mundane, and inspirational to make sure this book was published.

My editor and designer, Erika, whose enthusiasm truly brought this book to life.

To my mom whose love and nourishment is constant, fierce, inspired and childlike all at the same time. You and dad were always the salt of the earth and inspired delight to me. Sundays with you and being on the place are my honor.

To dad, now in spirit, for your encouragement, words of wisdom, your gritty, tender and unflinching love, wondering when my book would be done, and our endless laughter. I do miss the look that we shared and laughter till we couldn't breathe. But alas, it is still in my mind's eye making me laugh spontaneously till people wonder what the heck is going on, which of course, makes me laugh more.

To Merle, for the countless intuitive banterings that had nothing to do directly with what I was writing. Yet, no doubt, contributed to what would flow through me for inspiration. Here's to you my dear, wise, and deeply sensitive friend. See you someday on the other side. For now, I feel you.

For my friends Anita, Jes, Dottie, Bonnie, Mark and more who are the rich love of family in my life. For John, who in a smooth cloud of evening cigar and banter on the river would ask, how's your book coming along?

To my sailor and dear friend, Mike, our many hours on the water in silence, high winds, heeled over, double reefed, and drifting are woven through this book.

About the Author

Shelley Hawkins, MS, creator of The Self Connection, Inc., is an intuitive business advisor, author, and educator who has invested in the freedom and potentials of entrepreneurs, executives, visionary individuals and their teams for a couple decades. She is known for her ability to merge the mystical with the practical with extraordinary results. She guides her clients to lead intentional, expansive lives discovering their unlimited potentials and dissolving the obstacles within and around them. Her approach is highly effective across business operations and leadership—profitability, fulfillment, enhancing intuitive strategies, and creating cohesive cultural dynamics, for example—as well as client's personal goals of transformation in relationships, finances and health. "My primary intention is to love life. To guide people to lead and author their lives from their deepest freedom and highest aspirations, weaving their infinite nature throughout their everyday lives."

Notes

Notes

Notes

Notes

Notes

Made in the USA
Las Vegas, NV
21 June 2024

91336857R00131